KT-132-244

Withdrawn from Stock
Dublin City Public Libraries

Ancient Egyptian Civilization

Mummies
of Ancient Egypt

by Brianna Hall

Leabharlanna Poiblí Chathair Baile Átha Cliath
Dublin City Public Libraries

raintree
a Capstone company — publishers for children

Raintree is an imprint of Capstone Global Library Limited, a company incorporated in England and Wales having its registered office at 264 Banbury Road, Oxford, OX2 7DY – Registered company number: 6695582

www.raintree.co.uk
myorders@raintree.co.uk

Text © Capstone Global Library Limited 2016
The moral rights of the proprietor have been asserted.

All rights reserved. No part of this publication may be reproduced in any form or by any means (including photocopying or storing it in any medium by electronic means and whether or not transiently or incidentally to some other use of this publication) without the written permission of the copyright owner, except in accordance with the provisions of the Copyright, Designs and Patents Act 1988 or under the terms of a licence issued by the Copyright Licensing Agency, Saffron House, 6–10 Kirby Street, London EC1N 8TS (www.cla.co.uk). Applications for the copyright owner's written permission should be addressed to the publisher.

Edited by Mari Bolte
Designed by Juliette Peters
Picture research by Svetlana Zhurkin
Production by Laura Manthe

ISBN 978 1 4747 1727 4
19 18 17 16 15
10 9 8 7 6 5 4 3 2 1

British Library Cataloguing in Publication Data
A full catalogue record for this book is available from the British Library.

Photo Credits
Alamy: The Art Gallery Collection, 21; Bridgeman Art Library: Louvre, Paris, France/Christian Larrieu, 9; Corbis: Bettmann, 10, Gianni Dagli Orti, 11, National Geographic Society, 16; Getty Images: Patrick Landmann, 20; Library of Congress, 4; National Geographic Stock: Christopher Klein, 18, Kenneth Garrett, 13, 14–15, 22, 29; Newscom: AFP/Getty Images/Khaled Desouki, 23, akg-images/Coll. B. Garrett, 5, akg-images/François Guénet, 6, EPA/Khaled El-Fiqi, 27, EPA/Mike Nelson, 26; Shutterstock: artform (hieroglyphs), throughout, Brian Maudsley, 7, Fedor Selivanov (fact box frame), throughout, Mikhail Dudarev (pyramids), cover and throughout, Rafa Irusta (papyrus background), throughout, R-studio (background texture), cover and throughout, Studio 37, cover (front), Zbynek Burival, 25

We would like to thank Jennifer Houser Wegner, PhD, for her invaluable help in the preparation of this book.

Every effort has been made to contact copyright holders of material reproduced in this book. Any omissions will be rectified in subsequent printings if notice is given to the publisher.

All the internet addresses (URLs) given in this book were valid at the time of going to press. However, due to the dynamic nature of the internet, some addresses may have changed, or sites may have changed or ceased to exist since publication. While the author and publisher regret any inconvenience this may cause readers, no responsibility for any such changes can be accepted by either the author or the publisher.

Printed and bound in China.

CONTENTS

Leabharlann na Cabraí
Cabra Library
Tel: 8691414

Chapter 1

An amazing discovery

It was a hot day in July 1881, near the Valley of the Kings in Egypt. German **archaeologist** Émile Brugsch lowered himself into a cave. Blinking from the sudden shift to darkness, he saw dozens of shadowy shapes. It only took him a moment to realize he stood in a **tomb** full of mummies.

Coffins were propped against the wall. There were more on the floor, stacked on top of one another. There were also jars, statues, pots, texts, tools and jewellery.

Brugsch's tomb site, 1902.

archaeologist scientist who studies how people lived in the past

tomb grave, room or building that holds a dead body

Studying Egyptian mummies became popular in the late 1800s.

Brugsch and his team found 50 mummies and nearly 6,000 objects that day. The find became known as the Deir el Bahri **cache**. Before the discovery, Europeans had only read about the pharaohs. Now they could see mummies up close. A craze for Egyptian culture swept the continent. People couldn't get enough of the gods, **pharaohs** and mummies of ancient Egypt.

cache hidden place where something is stored

pharaoh king of ancient Egypt

Chapter 2

Preparing for the afterlife

The ancient Egyptians believed that everyone was born with a ba and a ka. The ba was the person's character, or personality. The ka was the person's life force. When a person died, their ba and ka separated. The ba could go to the **underworld**, but the ka stayed with the person's body. If the person's body was destroyed, their ka would be lost.

Tutankhamun (centre) and his ka (right) are greeted by the god Osiris.

underworld resting place of spirits who had died

To the ancient Egyptians, death was simply an interruption before reaching the next stage in life. Going from life to the afterlife was tricky. The ancient Egyptians believed that all parts of the person must be kept whole – body, spirit and name. They also chanted spells after a person's death. They believed the special words gave the person's ka courage, wit and strength.

What's in a name?

The Egyptians believed a person's name was important. If a person died without their name written down, they would not go on to the afterlife. Names were recorded on pieces of **papyrus**, on statues and on tomb walls. Priests and family members honoured the person's name with spells.

The pharaoh Hatshepsut's name, carved into stone.

papyrus writing material made from plants

Chapter 3

Making a mummy

Making a mummy was a long process. A priest called the Overseer of Mysteries was in charge. He directed ceremonies and read the chants that protected the dead person's ka.

Priests who performed the **mummification** wore masks. They wanted to look like Anubis, the god of **embalming** and mummification. If the priests did a good job, the mummy would enjoy the afterlife. If not, the person's ka would be lost forever.

After the body was washed with oil and wine, the internal organs were removed. Workers called bandagers cut a hole in the side of the body. Then they removed the internal organs. All the organs, except the heart, were placed in **canopic jars**. Egyptians believed that the mummies would have their organs returned to them in the afterlife.

mummification process of making a mummy to preserve a dead person's body

embalming preserving a dead body so it does not decay

canopic jar jar that held the organs of a dead person

A heavy heart

The ancient Egyptians believed that a person's heart was the key to the afterlife. In death, protective charms were often placed over the mummy's heart. In the afterlife, gods weighed the dead person's heart on a set of scales. People who led good lives had hearts that balanced on the scales. They entered paradise. A demon called Amamet ate the hearts of those who tipped the scales. Then the unworthy person entered a world of fire forever.

Each canopic jar was protected by a son of the god Horus. Each god guarded a specific organ.

Duamutef
stomach

Imsety
liver

Qebehsenuef
intestines

Hapy
lungs

Embalmers and a coffin decorator.

Next the body was dried. Bandagers used a salt-like substance called natron. The natron was piled all over the body. Embalmers also filled the inside of the body with natron. Over the next 40 days, the body lost 75 per cent of its original weight. Another 30 days were spent wrapping the mummy in bandages.

Workers stuffed the mummy with packing material, such as rags or sawdust. The stuffing helped the body look fuller and more lifelike. Spices and oils, such as cinnamon and myrrh, made the body smell nice. A coat of resin or beeswax kept pests away.

FACT

Wrapping the dead in linen turned the body into a house for the ka.

Small charms called **amulets** were placed in the mummy's wrappings and on the body. These charms protected both the living and the dead.

The shape and colour of each amulet were important. Green or blue amulets symbolized rebirth. Red stood for energy or power. Popular shapes included animals, symbols based on **hieroglyphs** or gods.

Small statues, called shabtis, were often included at burial sites. These figures would help the dead person in the afterlife. They were there to do undesirable work, such as farming or building things. Most tombs contained between one and 10 shabtis. Some tombs had a shabti for every day of the year.

FACT

King Tut was buried with more than 140 amulets.

amulet small charm believed to protect the wearer from harm

hieroglyphs pictures or symbols used in the ancient Egyptian system of writing

Mummies were placed inside coffins for burial. Early coffins were very plain. Towards the end of the Old Kingdom (2625–2130 BC), they began decorating the inside of the coffin with words. These writings were called coffin texts. Egyptians believed that these spells would help the dead pass safely into the afterlife.

Rich Egyptians employed artists to decorate their coffins with golden paint, pictures and protective spells. Some coffins were painted with maps of the underworld. The map would ensure the person's spirit would not get lost. Others were painted with protective symbols, such as eyes, wings or gods. Poor people bought simple, pre-made coffins.

The mummies of the richest Egyptians were placed inside several coffins. Sometimes the coffins were human-shaped and decorated with gold paint, coloured glass and hieroglyphs. Coffins of pharaohs and other important people were placed inside a large stone case called a **sarcophagus**.

sarcophagus stone coffin

FACT

Today's scholars disagree about the order of pharaohs, family kingdoms and dynasties. Over time, the keeping of records became disorganized. Some records have been lost.

The inner and outer sarcophagi of the mummy Iufaa.

FACT

Iufaa's mummy was buried in a wooden coffin. The coffin lay inside an inner sarcophagus made of basalt. The outer sarcophagus was made of limestone. It weighed 49 tonnes.

Tombs and pyramids

Most mummies were buried in tombs. These "houses of eternity" had two sections. An underground chamber held the coffin and the mummy's burial goods. An offering place chapel was above ground. There, the living asked the dead for help or advice. They wrote their wishes on scrolls so the dead could read them.

The tomb and chapel could be simple or complex, depending on the person's importance. Pharaohs and other rich people built tombs of quarried stone. These huge tombs were expensive and took years to finish. Poorer people either made small tombs of mud brick or buried coffins directly in the sand.

Tombs became bigger and more elaborate around 2700 BC. Pharaoh Djoser wished to demonstrate his power and wealth. He built Egypt's first pyramid tomb, the Step Pyramid, near Cairo. The Step Pyramid still stands today. It has six tiers and is roughly 60 metres (200 feet) high.

Pictures of the underworld were painted on the walls of Amenhotep II's tomb.

Less than a hundred years later, Pharaoh Khufu built the Great Pyramid of Giza. This huge tomb is made up of more than 2.3 million blocks of limestone. It weighs an estimated 6.3 million tonnes.

Djoser, Khufu and other pharaohs wanted to continue enjoying the luxuries they experienced on Earth. They believed large, beautiful tombs would help them maintain their royal status in the afterlife.

Chapter 4

Burials

With the body prepared and the tomb built, the mummy could be put to rest. Priests and family members walked to the burial site. Richer people hired professional mourners. The mourners cried and beat their chests with grief.

Women performed a ceremonial dance at the burial site. Things such as furniture, weapons, jewellery and the canopic jars were placed in the tomb. Food was brought for the mummy to eat in the afterlife.

The path to the afterlife

Ancient Egyptians believed the path to the afterlife was full of dangers, such as monsters and riddles. To help the spirits, priests wrote a sort of guide to the underworld. The collection of spells was known as the *Book of the Dead*.

These scrolls were very expensive. Scribes wrote every word by hand on papyrus. Rich Egyptians could afford their own copy of the text. These scrolls were buried with the mummies. Poor people had phrases from the text carved onto their coffin or simply spoken before burial.

Before the mummy could be buried, a **ritual** called the opening of the mouth took place. The ceremony had more than 75 steps and was performed by an official called a sem-priest. The sem-priest touched an adze, a type of carpenter's tool, to the mummy's face. This process would help the mummy see, speak, eat and move in the afterlife.

After the ceremony, a final prayer was said. Then the mummy was buried. Mourners then held a feast near the tomb.

ritual action that is always done the same way

17

Chapter 5

Famous mummies

For years, pharaohs were buried in pyramids located in northern Egypt. Many were buried near the Giza Plateau. However, during the New Kingdom (1539–1075 BC), the pharaohs moved south to the Valley of the Kings. More than 60 tombs of New Kingdom rulers are located in the valley.

A cutaway view of Seti I's tomb in the Valley of the Kings.

It took how long?

Building a tomb was a long process that could take a lifetime to complete. Hundreds of builders, artists and scribes were needed. During the New Kingdom, workers and their families lived near the Valley of the Kings. They were the only people who knew the location of the valley, also called the Place of Truth. Secrecy helped protect the tombs from grave robbers.

Valley of the Kings

Each tomb in the Valley of the Kings has an official KV (Kings' Valley) number.

East Valley

Deir el Bahri cache

Nile River

N
W   E
S

Famous Tombs (KV Name)
- Hatshepsut - KV20
- Rameses II - KV7
- Tiye - KV35
- The Younger Lady - KV35
- Seti I - KV17
- Tutankhamun - KV62

Pharaoh Seti I

Rule: 1294 or 1290–1279 BC
Discovered: 1881
Original tomb location:
Valley of the Kings (KV17)
Tomb uncovered:
Deir el Bahri cache

Seti I was a successful and respected pharaoh. But his reign was a short one. He began many building projects that were not completed in his lifetime.

Seti planned a long, deep tomb in the Valley of the Kings. It was cut into hundreds of feet of rock. A well was built into the tomb to keep flood waters from ruining the tomb. It would also trap careless grave robbers.

The tomb was beautifully decorated with detailed scenes and writings. Religious texts and magical spells lined the walls and pillars of the tomb. Large paintings showed scenes of the gods and the underworld. His sarcophagus was covered with hieroglyphs and carvings.

When the tomb was first explored in 1817, archaeologists noticed that Seti's mummy was missing. Decades later, the pharaoh's mummy was found at the royal cache in Deir el Bahri. Priests probably moved the mummy to protect it from grave robbers.

Pharaoh Rameses II

Rule: 1279–1212 BC
Discovered: 1881
Original tomb location:
Valley of the Kings (KV7)
Tomb uncovered:
Deir el Bahri cache

Also known as Rameses the Great, the son of Seti I ruled for 66 years. He was one of the longest-reigning pharaohs. He was also one of the oldest, living to 92. He had eight wives and at least 100 children. His large family gave him the nickname The Great Ancestor.

Rameses was originally buried in the Valley of the Kings. His tomb spans more than 820 square metres (8,800 square feet). It is one of the largest in the valley. His temple, called the Ramesseum, is also large, at 300 metres (984 feet) long and 195 metres (640 feet) wide.

Unfortunately, the tomb did not stand the test of time. Flood waters ruined the paintings. Thieves also broke into his tomb and stole its valuables. Priests moved his mummy to keep it safe. It was first moved in 1054 BC, to Seti I's resting place. It was later moved again to the Deir el Bahri cache.

Queen Tiye, the "Elder Lady"

Queen: 1389–1338 BC
Discovered: 1898
Original tomb location:
Valley of the Kings (KV35)

Queen Tiye married the pharaoh Amenhotep III at a very young age. Her husband loved her dearly. The two were often shown together in paintings and statues. She helped Amenhotep make decisions in court about war and trade. Her face was carved onto a sphinx statue, an honour usually reserved for pharaohs. After her husband died, Tiye acted as an adviser to her son, Akhenaten.

Archaeologists found Tiye's mummy in a tomb with more than a dozen other royals. Her body was unwrapped and unmarked. Some believe the mummies were moved to protect them from grave robbers.

For a century, scholars called this unknown mummy the "Elder Lady". They guessed her identity after some of her long, red hair was found in Tutankhamun's tomb. The hair was in a small coffin marked with her name.

In 2010, DNA tests proved that the mummy was Tiye. Scientists had already taken the DNA of Tiye's parents, Yuya and Tuyu. After taking the Elder Lady's DNA, they were finally able to identify the lost queen.

The "Younger Lady"

Lived: circa 1340 BC
Discovered: 1898
Original tomb location:
Valley of the Kings (KV35)

Her name is unknown, and her story is full of mystery. This mummy was found alongside the Elder Lady. Scientists called her the "Younger Lady".

For years, historians debated who the mummy could have been. For a long time, people thought she was either Queen Nefertiti or Princess Kiya. Both were wives of Pharaoh Akhenaten. In 2010, scientists took DNA from a number of mummies. They were shocked by what they learnt. The Younger Lady was one of pharaoh Akhenaten's five known sisters. She was also the mother of his son, Tutankhamun.

FACT

Ancient Egyptians believed that gods could only marry other gods. Sometimes this meant they married their siblings. Because pharaohs were seen as earthly gods, this practice was common among Egyptian royal families too.

How were they connected?

In 2010, scientists took DNA samples from 11 mummies. They looked at the mummies' genetic markers to work out family lines. Certain markers are passed from parents to children. Scientists compared these markers with previously established information, such as ruling periods and tomb writings. They were able to draw a family tree that started with Yuya and Tuyu and ended with Tutankhamun.

Pharaoh Tutankhamun

Rule: 1333–1323 BC
Discovered: 1922
Original tomb location:
Valley of the Kings (KV62)

Pharaoh Tutankhamun is the best-known Egyptian ruler. He became pharaoh when he was nine years old. He died 10 years later.

King Tut is not famous for his reign or his lifestyle. He is famous because of his tomb. His small tomb in the Valley of the Kings remained untouched for more than 3,000 years. Howard Carter uncovered the tomb in 1922. He found more than 5,000 artefacts. The discovery fascinated the world.

It took 10 years to remove, clean and document all of the objects. Today, Tut's mummy still rests in the Valley of the Kings. Instead of resting in its gold sarcophagus, it now lies in a climate-controlled container. This glass box protects the mummy from further damage.

FACT

Tut's golden burial mask stands nearly 0.6 metres (2 feet) tall. It is decorated with gold, glass and precious stones.

Pharaoh Hatshepsut

Rule: 1479–1457 BC
Discovered: 1903
Original tomb location:
Valley of the Kings (KV20)
Tomb uncovered:
Valley of the Kings

Pharaoh Hatshepsut was the longest reigning female pharaoh. She was also one of the few female leaders. She built complex temples and statues for the royal family and the gods. Even though she was a woman, statues and paintings show her wearing the symbols of a male pharaoh, such as a false beard or a man's crown and clothing. Some writings even refer to her as "he" or "him".

Hatshepsut's tomb in the Valley of the Kings was 200 metres (656 ft) long. However, when the tomb was discovered in 1903, there were no mummies to be found. The sarcophagus inside was empty and unused.

Later, the tomb of Hatshepsut's nurse was found near by. There were two female mummies inside. Scientists thought one might be Hatshepsut. But because there was no way to identify the body, they left it in the tomb. The mummy was finally removed and positively identified as Hatshepsut in 2007.

Animal mummies

Millions of animal mummies dating back to ancient Egypt lay buried in the sands. Crocodiles, birds, baboons and cats were the most common animals made into mummies.

Some animal mummies were made to serve as sources of food in the afterlife. Others were meant to be pets.

The people of ancient Egypt believed that certain animals represented certain gods. In the early days of Egyptian civilization, each town was represented by an animal. These animals were much like modern sports mascots. When a person became pharaoh, their town animal was given the status of a god.

Portrait mummies

Romans took control of Egypt in 30 BC. This change in rule also changed mummy making. Less time was spent preserving the body and more time was spent decorating it. Mummies were wrapped in a criss-cross pattern. Lifelike portraits were painted on wood and placed over the mummy's face. The faces were realistic and did not contain religious symbols. Portrait mummies were some of the last mummies made in Egypt.

Leabharlanna Poiblí Chathair Baile Átha Cliath
Dublin City Public Libraries

Chapter 6

Mummies today

By studying mummies, scientists can learn more about how ancient Egyptians lived. A hundred years ago, people learnt about mummies by unwrapping them. After the mummies were taken apart and studied, they were usually thrown away.

Wild mummy uses

Would you go to a mummy unwrapping party? The first party of this type took place in the 1500s. However, they did not become popular until the 1900s. Rich men would buy mummies in secret and invite their friends round. Unwrapping a mummy was a frightening and unique form of entertainment.

Once the fun was over, the wrappings and body parts were sold or thrown away. Peddlers would crush the dusty linen and dry mummies to use as medicine. They claimed the powder had healing powers.

Today, scientists and historians use X-ray machines, scans and chemical analysis to study mummies. Studying mummies closely teaches them how ancient Egyptians worked, what they ate and how they died.

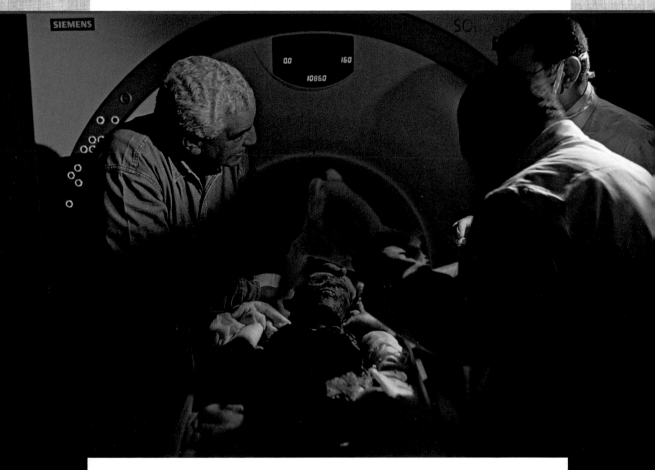

Ancient Egypt has fascinated historians and scientists for generations. They believe that mummies provide a window into this past civilization. Scientists continue to unwrap the mystery of the mummy. As more mummies are discovered, researchers will continue to uncover more secrets of the ancient world.

GLOSSARY

amulet small charm believed to protect the wearer from harm

archaeologist scientist who studies how people lived in the past

cache hidden place where something is stored

canopic jar jar that held the organs of a dead person

embalming preserving a dead body so it does not decay

hieroglyphs pictures or symbols used in the ancient Egyptian system of writing

mummification process of making a mummy to preserve a dead person's body

papyrus writing material made from plants

pharaoh king of ancient Egypt

ritual action that is always done the same way

sarcophagus stone coffin

tomb grave, room or building that holds a dead body

underworld resting place of spirits who had died

Ancient Egypt (History Detective Investigates), Rachel Minay (Wayland, 2014)

Ancient Egyptians (Explore!), Jane Bingham (Wayland, 2015)

Egyptian Myths and Legends (All About Myths), Fiona Macdonald (Raintree, 2013)

WEBSITES

www.ancientegypt.co.uk/mummies/home.html
Learn all about mummies and the mummification process in ancient Egypt.

www.bbc.co.uk/history/ancient/egyptians
Discover cool facts about hieroglyphs, mummification, gods and goddesses and more.

Leabharlanna Poiblí Chathair Baile Átha Cliath
Dublin City Public Libraries